EXPLORING THE CATHOLIC FAITH

A GUIDE THROUGH THE BASICS

Herbert McCabe, O.P.

Foreword by Timothy Radcliffe, O.P.

BOOKS & MEDIA
Boston

Nihil Obstat: Rev. Thomas W. Buckley, STD, SSL
Imprimatur: ✠ Seán Cardinal O'Malley, O.F.M. Cap.
Archbishop of Boston
October 18, 2007

Library of Congress Cataloging-in-Publication Data

McCabe, Herbert, 1926–2001
Exploring the Catholic faith : a guide through the basics / Herbert McCabe ; foreword by Timothy Radcliffe.— USA ed.
p. cm.
Includes index.
ISBN 0-8198-2361-9 (pbk.)
1. Catholic Church—Doctrines. 2. Theology, Doctrinal—Popular works. I. Title.
BX1754.M155 2008
282—dc22

2007035422

Cover design by Rosana Usselmann

Cover photo: angusimages.com

First published in Great Britain in 1985 by The Incorporated Catholic Truth Society

Revised edition published by Darton, Longman and Todd, London, UK

Published by Pauline Books & Media, 50 Saint Paul's Avenue, Boston, MA 02130-3491. www.pauline.org.

Printed in the U.S.A.

Pauline Books & Media is the publishing house of the Daughters of St. Paul, an international congregation of women religious serving the Church with the communications media.

1 2 3 4 5 6 7 8 9 12 11 10 09 08

Contents

Part Three

LIFE IN THE SPIRIT

Foreword

This catechism is a wonderful book. It offers a clear presentation of the principal teachings of the Catholic Church, which will be instructive and stimulating for everyone, whether they know nothing about Christianity or want to learn more. It is ecumenical and unpolemical in tone.

It is, like some earlier catechisms, written in the form of questions and answers. This may appear to be a strange way to write a book, but it recognizes that we learn by asking questions, and we progress not only by finding the answers but also by discovering new and better questions. Herbert McCabe was a brilliant teacher because he clearly stated the Church's answers not only to the questions that everyone puts, but also to the questions that we had never thought of. A book which answers questions could give the impression of complacency. It might wrongly suggest that if we read this book, then all our questions will be answered and our doubts resolved, and we need never reflect upon our faith again. Nothing could be further from McCabe's intention.

The Catholic Church does teach, and he attempts to expound that teaching clearly and faithfully, but that teaching always draws us nearer to the mystery of God, which transcends all knowledge. These questions and answers invite us to undertake the pilgrimage toward the mystery, and on the way to face new questions of our own.

The answers are given as simply as possible. This is not because they are superficial. Having lived with Herbert McCabe for more than twenty years, I know that this simplicity is the fruit of deep study, reflection, and prayer. One has to be a very good theologian indeed to write so simply. This simplicity is appropriate for a book that talks about God, whose dazzling simplicity is beyond our grasp. All human growth draws us beyond duplicity and self-contradiction, toward that divine simplicity.

This presentation of Christian doctrine is wonderfully humane, and that is because Christianity embodies God's invitation to us to flourish. It tells us of God who "wants each kind of creature to flourish in the way appropriate to it, and he wants his human creatures not only to flourish in a human way but to share his own life and happiness forever" (q. 2). The deep humanity of our faith marks the treatment of every question. For example, the virtue of chastity is not described, as so often, only in terms of what one is not permitted to do, but also includes "being warm and affectionate...to others" (q. 243). Every time I have gone back to this little book, I have been stimulated and illuminated, and discovered new ways in which the Gospel is indeed good news for all human beings.

TIMOTHY RADCLIFFE, O.P.
Former Master of the Order of Preachers

Introduction

This catechism is not intended to be a substitute for a catechist. It is meant to provide guidelines and a framework for questions that catechist and inquirer may discuss together. In many cases the answers are so designed as naturally to give rise to further questions. Just how deeply the matter should then be pursued is something the catechist must decide in a particular case. It is hoped that the catechism will be useful to the catechist at many different levels of instruction, both for children and for adult inquirers.

Inevitably the book invites comparison with the older *Catechism of Christian Doctrine* (Catholic Truth Society, London, 1889), which is still in use in the United Kingdom. The first difference is that in this book the answers are not designed to be learned by heart and so, while I have aimed at brevity, I have not achieved the lapidary character of the earlier work. As to content, the main differences are that here the mystery of the Trinity permeates the entire teaching; secondly, the sacraments are treated not simply as channels of grace but as constitutive of the life of the Church; and, thirdly, I have abandoned the sixteenth-century innovation of dealing with the moral life in terms of the commandments and how they may be broken, and returned to an earlier tradition that explains the virtues and how they may be cultivated throughout one's whole life.

I have tried not to side with any particular theological school, but the influence of St. Thomas Aquinas will be obvious enough, and I hope that this catechism bears somewhat the same relation to the Second Vatican Council as the earlier one did to the Council of Trent.

HERBERT MCCABE, O.P.
Blackfriars
Oxford

Part One

The Redemption

God and His Love for Us

1 *Why is God called Creator?*

God is called Creator because he[1] made everything there is and holds it all continually in being.

2 *What does God want for his creatures?*

God wants each kind of creature to flourish in the way appropriate to it, and he wants his human creatures not only to flourish in a human way but to share his own life and happiness forever.

3 *Does belief in creation mean rejecting evolution or other scientific accounts of the origins of things?*

It does not, for creation and scientific explanation are answers to different questions. Science seeks to answer the question: "What kind of world do we have?" while creation is the answer to the question: "Why is there a world (of any kind) rather than nothing at all?"

4 *How are we to think of God?*

We are not to think of God as a powerful being within the universe but as Creator of the entire universe and all that is in it. We are to thank him for the gift of our lives and for all the love he has shown us. We are to obey his law, which will lead to happiness with him.

5 *How has God shown his love for us?*

God has shown his love for us by giving us our lives but even more by forgiving us when we disobeyed him, and raising us up to share in his own life through Jesus Christ. This is called our redemption.

The Promise of the Redeemer

6 *How does the Bible tell the story of our redemption?*

The Bible begins the story of our redemption with the first promise of a Redeemer in Genesis 3:15; this passage is called the Protoevangelium (or first Gospel). The Bible then describes God's call to Abraham nearly four thousand years ago, when God promised to make him the ancestor of a great people who would bring God's blessing on the whole world. Abraham believed the word of God: this was the beginning of faith.

7 *What, in the Bible story, happened to Abraham's people?*

Abraham's people, the Hebrews or Israelites, were enslaved in Egypt for four hundred years; but God raised up Moses to deliver them from slavery and to lead them through the waters of the sea toward the Promised Land. This is called the Exodus. It is celebrated annually in the Paschal (or Passover) feast.

8 *What did God do for his people after the Exodus?*

After the Exodus, God gave his people a rule of life called the Law, which is summed up in the Ten Commandments. They were to abandon the false gods and to live in justice and peace with each other according to his Law.

9 *What are the Ten Commandments?*

God said: I am the Lord your God, who brought you out of slavery:

You shall have no gods except me...
You shall not speak the name of the Lord to misuse it;
Keep the Sabbath day holy;
Honor your father and your mother;
You shall not kill;
You shall not commit adultery;

You shall not steal;
You shall not testify falsely against your neighbor;
You shall not covet your neighbor's wife;
You shall not covet your neighbor's possessions
(see Ex 20:1–18).

10 *What do the commandments principally show us?*

The commandments principally show us the basic requirements for a life of friendship with God and with each other.

11 *Did the Israelites, the people of God, reach the Promised Land?*

They reached the Promised Land and eventually, under King David (c. 1000 B.C.), entered the city of Jerusalem. David was promised that his family would rule the people of God forever.

12 *How was this promise to David fulfilled?*

The promise to David was fulfilled in his descendant, Jesus, who is Christ[2] the King for ever.

13 *In the Bible story, what happened to the people of God after the reign of David?*

After the reign of David, most of their kings were corrupt and fell away from the law of the Lord. They were conquered and taken into exile for seventy years in Babylon (c. 600 B.C.).

14 *Who were the prophets?*

The prophets were people who, around this time, spoke the word of God, warning Israel against unfaithfulness but speaking often of her great destiny and the future coming of the Savior.

15 *Who were the major prophets?*

The major prophets, so called because so many of their prophecies have been preserved, were Isaiah, Jeremiah, Ezekiel, and Daniel.

16 *What happened to the people of God after the Exile?*

In Judea, the returned exiles, now known as the Jews, living in peace, were able to develop the Law and ideas of personal responsibility and destiny, especially belief in the resurrection. During this time some parts of the Bible were written, such as the Wisdom literature and the Book of Daniel.

17 *Who was the promised Savior?*

The promised Savior was the Jewish prophet Jesus, the son of Mary, of the line of David, who was born in Bethlehem, the city of David, two thousand years ago.

The Redeemer: Jesus Christ

18 *Who is Jesus?*

Jesus is the eternal Son of God who became truly and completely human in the womb of Mary while remaining truly and completely divine. He is more human than we are for he is "like to us in all things except sin" (Heb 4:15), for, because of sin, we are less than fully human.

19 *What do we call the mystery of the true humanity and true divinity of the one person, Jesus?*

The mystery of the true humanity and true divinity of Jesus is called the Incarnation.

20 *What do the Gospels of Matthew and Luke say about the parentage of Jesus?*

The Gospels of Matthew and Luke say that Jesus had no earthly father but was born of the Virgin Mary, who conceived him by the power of the Holy Spirit.

21 *When do we celebrate the conception and birth of Jesus?*

We celebrate the conception of Jesus on the feast of the Annunciation (March 25), and his birth on Christmas Day (December 25).

Jesus, His Father, and the Holy Spirit

22 *What did Jesus preach?*

Jesus preached the coming of the kingdom, or reign, of God.

23 *What did Jesus principally teach us about God?*

Jesus taught that God is our Father who loves us; he taught that God was his Father in a special way. Jesus, the eternal Son of God, wanted us to be joined with him in this special sonship by enabling us to be adopted as God's children.

24 *How are we joined with Jesus in his sonship to the Father?*

We are joined to Jesus as Son of the Father by receiving the Holy Spirit.

25 *What do we mean by God the Father?*

By God the Father we mean God as eternally begetting the Son (or conceiving the Word), and as eternally breathing forth the Spirit.

26 *What do we mean by God the Son?*

By God the Son we mean God as eternally begotten by the Father and as eternally breathing forth the Spirit.

27 *What do we mean by God the Holy Spirit?*

By God the Holy Spirit we mean God as eternally breathed forth by the Father and the Son.

28 *What has the eternal conceiving of the Word to do with our redemption?*

In sending us the Word made flesh, the Father is sharing with us the word or concept in which he himself eternally understands his divine life.

29 *What has the eternal breathing forth of the Spirit to do with our redemption?*

By the grace which we receive, the Father through the Son is sharing with us the Holy Spirit who is his own eternal enjoyment of the divine life.

30 *Are Father, Son, and Holy Spirit three Gods?*

Father, Son, and Holy Spirit are not three Gods but three Persons who are distinct from each other by their relationship with each other within the one Godhead. This mystery of the three Persons who are one God is called the Trinity.

31 *How is the mystery of the Trinity revealed to us?*

The mystery of the Trinity is revealed to us as we meditate in faith on the deepest meaning of the life, death, resurrection, and ascension of Jesus: the mysteries of Christmas, Easter, and Pentecost.

32 *In the story of Jesus, how is the eternal coming forth of the Word from the Father revealed to us?*

Jesus was sent to us by his Father to share totally our human life and was obedient to this mission. In faith, we recognize the sending of Jesus by his Father in our history as the image or sacrament of the coming forth of the Word from the Father in eternity.

33 *In the story of Jesus, how is the eternal coming forth of the Spirit revealed to us?*

Jesus was raised from the dead and ascended to be with his Father. Through Jesus, the Father poured forth the Spirit upon the world at Pentecost. In faith, we recognize the outpouring of the Spirit through Jesus in our history as the image or sacrament of the coming forth of the Spirit from the Father through the Son in eternity.

34 *Are the Son and the Spirit created by the Father?*

No. Although the Son owes his being to the Father, and the Spirit owes his being to the Father through the Son, they are not creatures but co-equal and co-eternal with the Father. For this reason Jesus, the Son of God made man, is truly divine, and the Spirit we have received through him is also truly divine.

35 *What do we call our receiving of the Holy Spirit by which we are joined to Jesus as children of the Father and thus share the divine life?*

We call this receiving of the Holy Spirit sanctifying grace.

36 *Can we deserve to receive the Holy Spirit by any merits or works of our own?*

We cannot deserve to receive the Holy Spirit for we are only creatures, and sinful creatures at that. The Spirit is given to us freely by the Father out of his great love for us. But once we have begun to live by the Spirit, our own works may deserve increased grace in this life and the joys of life in heaven.

37 *Does living by the Spirit mean that we no longer act freely of ourselves?*

It does not, for God our Creator is the source of our freedom and it is by his continual creative act that we have our own lives and our own free activity; so his life and activity within us can never be a rival or alternative to our own life and activity.

38 *What did Jesus tell us about living the life of the Spirit?*

Jesus told us about life in the Spirit when he taught the Beatitudes:

Blessed are the poor in spirit, for theirs is the kingdom of heaven.
Blessed are those who mourn, for they shall be comforted.
Blessed are the meek, for they shall inherit the earth.
Blessed are those who hunger and thirst for what is right, for they shall be satisfied.
Blessed are the merciful, for they shall obtain mercy.
Blessed are the pure in heart, for they shall see God.
Blessed are the peacemakers, for they shall be called children of God.
Blessed are those who are persecuted for the sake of what is right, for theirs is the kingdom of heaven (Mt 5:3–10).

Crucifixion, Resurrection, Pentecost

39 *Was Jesus himself persecuted for the sake of what is right?*

Jesus was persecuted for the sake of what is right: he was arrested, tried by his own religious leaders and by the state, condemned, tortured, and put to death on the cross.

40 *Why did the authorities put Jesus to death?*

They put him to death because his teaching that people should live by love for each other and his certainty of his own authority led him to set aside certain laws and customs (which he described as "the tradition of men" rather than the commandment of God; Mk 7:8), and even to disrupt the activities of the Temple. This seemed to the leaders of his own people a threat to both religion and society and so led the Roman government to regard him as subversive.

41 *Was Jesus opposed to law?*

Jesus was not opposed to law, but he taught that the law is only really obeyed when it is fulfilled as an expression of love.

42 *Who were the first followers and cooperators of Jesus?*

The first followers and cooperators of Jesus were the apostles, led by Peter, whom Jesus sent to preach in his name.

43 *Were the apostles always faithful to Jesus?*

They were not. One of them, Judas, betrayed Jesus to the authorities. When Jesus was arrested, the others forsook him and fled, and their leader, Peter, repeatedly disowned him.

44 *What did Jesus do when he knew he was about to be arrested?*

When he knew he was about to be arrested, Jesus celebrated a solemn paschal meal with the apostles. He gave them, under the form of bread and wine, his body and blood, which were to be sacrificed for them on the cross, to be their shared food and drink as a sign of their unity in the Spirit of love on earth and as a token of their future unity in the kingdom of heaven. This meal was called the Last Supper.

45 *What is a paschal meal?*

A paschal meal is a gathering that commemorates the liberation of the people of God from slavery in Egypt at the Exodus. The Last Supper commemorates the liberation of humankind from slavery to sin. This liberation begins in us in this world with our life in the Spirit and will be completed with the coming of the kingdom.

46 *Can we join with Jesus in his celebration of the Last Supper?*

We join with Jesus and with all his followers in his celebration of the Last Supper whenever we join in the celebration of Mass.

47 *On what days do we especially commemorate the Last Supper and the death of Jesus?*

We especially commemorate the Last Supper and the death of Jesus during Holy Week, on Holy Thursday and Good Friday.

48 *Why did Jesus submit to his death on the cross?*

Jesus submitted to his death on the cross because he wished to live out the full implications of being loving in a loveless world; he wished to accept the consequences of accepting sinners. In his death he fulfilled his mission from the Father and completed the task of living a truly human life, a task in which all others had failed. "Christ died for our sins in accordance with the scriptures" (I Cor 15:3).

49 *What does St. John's Gospel call the collective failure of humankind to be truly human?*

St. John calls the collective failure of humankind to be truly human the sin of the world.

50 *What do we call our congenital involvement in the sin of the world?*

We call our congenital involvement in the sin of the world original sin, because we are infected by it from our very origin when we are conceived as human (cf. q. 138). St. Paul speaks of this sin as a power present in fallen humanity (cf. Rom 5:12; 8:7–8).

51 *How does the Old Testament treat the sin of the world?*

The Book of Genesis tells the story of a primeval sin of our first parents, a disobedience by which they lost paradise for themselves and their descendants.

52 *Have we committed original sin?*

We have not personally committed original sin. It is an absence of grace and a moral weakness we suffer from that shows itself in the injustice of our society and in the actual personal sins we commit, but most characteristically in the murder of Jesus.

53 *How did God liberate us from original sin?*

God liberated us from original sin by sending his Son, Jesus, to take on all the consequences of being truly human, even to being killed by us on the cross, and, in response to this man's loving obedience, raising him up to be the first fruits of a new humanity to which we are joined by faith in him (cf. Phil 2:6–11).

54 *Is our liberation from original sin completed?*

Our liberation from original sin is not yet completed, for although by faith we are no longer enslaved by the sin of this world, we still suffer from it as from an enemy that we must overcome by grace. For this reason we still need to struggle for a more just society, and we are still subject to death and to temptation to personal sins.

55 *When will our liberation from original sin be completed?*

Our liberation will be completed at the second coming of Christ in glory on the last day. Then we shall be raised up to new life in the kingdom of justice, peace, and love; then both sin and death will finally be conquered.

56 *How did the liberation of humankind from sin and death first appear?*

The liberation of humankind from sin and death began with the resurrection of Jesus.

57 *What do we mean by the resurrection of Jesus?*

By the resurrection we mean that Jesus, having truly died, was raised from the dead by his Father on the third day to a new life of glory in the kingdom. For this reason his body was not to be found in the tomb, for, having conquered death, he now lives a new, immortal, human bodily life. In this life he appeared several times to his followers.

58 *When do we especially celebrate the resurrection of Jesus?*

We especially celebrate the resurrection in Holy Week at the Easter Vigil on Holy Saturday night and Easter Sunday, but every Sunday is also a celebration of the resurrection.

59 *When Jesus, risen from the dead, was reunited with his Father, what did they do?*

Jesus risen from the dead and reunited with his Father sent the Holy Spirit upon his followers.

60 *On what day do we especially celebrate the sending of the Holy Spirit?*

We especially celebrate the sending of the Holy Spirit on the day of Pentecost, the birthday of the Church.

Part Two

The Church

The Church and Tradition

61 *What is the Church?*

The Church is the community that, because it has received the Spirit, believes in Jesus, the Son of God, who through his sacrificial death on the cross brought salvation to the world. Through the faith of this community, the saving priestly act of Jesus, mediating between God and humanity, is brought to bear throughout history upon humankind.

62 *How is the Church to be recognized?*

The Church is to be recognized by her handing down through history the word of God and his sacraments.

63 *What is the handing down of the word and sacraments by the Church called?*

The handing down of the word and sacraments by the Church is called Tradition.

Scripture

64 *In the Tradition of the Church, where is the word of God principally to be found?*

In the Tradition of the Church, the word of God is principally to be found in the Scriptures (the Bible).

65 *What are the Scriptures?*

The Scriptures are the books of the Jewish Bible (the Old Testament) and the writings of the earliest Church (the New Testament): the letters of Paul and others; the Gospels of Mark, Matthew, and Luke, with the Book of Acts; the Gospel of John and the Book of the Apocalypse or Revelation.

66 *How are we to read the Scriptures?*

We are to read the Scriptures as the book of the Church: as the word of God in human words. We must try to understand what kind of human writings they are in order to understand what God is saying to us through them.

67 *What is the effect of listening to or reading the Scriptures?*

At one level, listening to or reading the Scriptures makes us understand better the story of God's love for us, the pre-history, history, and future of the Church. At another and deeper level, if we are properly disposed, it increases our faith by which we receive God's love for us, which is the outpouring of the Holy Spirit.

Sacraments

68 *What is a sacrament?*

A sacrament is a sacred sign by which we worship God, his love is revealed to us, and his saving work accomplished in us. In the sacraments, God shows us what he does and does what he shows us.

69 *What is the first sacrament?*

The first sacrament is the humanity of Jesus, "the image of the invisible God" (Col 1:15). The second is the Church herself, "the sacrament of union with God and of the unity of mankind" (*Lumen Gentium*, 1).

70 *What are the sacraments of the Church?*

The sacraments of the Church are: the Eucharist, Baptism, Confirmation, Holy Orders, Marriage, Penance, and the Anointing of the Sick.

71 *Are these sacraments prayers?*

These sacraments are the first and fundamental prayer of the Church by which we are joined to Christ in his prayer to the Father.

72 *What mysteries are revealed and enacted in the sacraments of the Church?*

In a sacrament of the Church there is revealed and enacted, firstly, a mystery of the Church herself, a realization in history of the priestly work of Christ; and, secondly, through this, a mystery of the kingdom, a mystery of the Spirit in each of us, a mystery of grace.

73 *Is a sacrament always effective?*

A sacrament genuinely celebrated always brings about the priestly mystery of the Church that it signifies and through this, in one who is properly disposed to receive the Spirit, the mystery of grace.

74 *Can we share in the mystery of grace without celebrating the sacrament?*

We can share in the Spirit, the mystery of grace, by our desire to receive the sacrament, even if the celebration is in some way prevented, but in such a case the mystery of the Church is not enacted.

The Eucharist

75 *What is the greatest sacrament of the Church?*

The greatest sacrament of the Church is the Eucharist: the sacred meal in which the unity of the Church in love is symbolized and effected; the sacrifice of Christ is recalled, made present, and offered; and the future unity of humankind in the kingdom is anticipated.

76 *What mystery of the Church is signified and brought about in the Eucharist?*

The mystery of the Church[3] that is signified and brought about in the Eucharist is the consecration of our offerings by which the body and blood of Christ our priest, sacrificed to be our spiritual food, is sacramentally present under the appearances of bread and wine.

77 *What mystery of grace is signified and brought about in the Eucharist?*

The mystery of grace (see n. 3, p. 91) that is signified and brought about in the Eucharist is the unity of Christ's followers in the Spirit of charity.

78 *When was the first Eucharist celebrated?*

The first Eucharist was celebrated at the Last Supper when Christ, before he was given up to death, a death he freely accepted, took bread and gave thanks and praise to his Father. He broke the bread, gave it to his disciples, and said: "Take this, all of you, and eat it; this is my body which will be given up for you." When supper was ended he took the cup; again he gave thanks and praise, gave the cup to his disciples, and said: "Take this, all of you, and drink from it. This is the cup of my blood, the blood of the new and everlasting covenant. It will be shed for you and for all, so that sins may be forgiven. Do this in memory of me."

79 *What happens to the bread and wine in the celebration of the Eucharist?*

In the celebration of the Eucharist, when the presiding priest repeats the words of Christ, by the power of the Holy Spirit the bread and wine are consecrated, cease to be bread and wine, and become the body and blood of Christ himself really present to us.

80 *When the consecrated bread is broken, or lifted up, or carried about, do these things happen to Christ himself?*

No. All such things happen only to the appearances by which Christ's presence is symbolized and effected.

81 *Is the Eucharist a sacrifice?*

The Eucharist is a sacrifice because in it the unique and all-sufficient sacrifice of Christ our priest is sacramentally represented and enacted.

82 *Why is it necessary for a priest of the Church to preside at the Eucharist?*

It is necessary for a priest to preside at the Eucharist because by ordination the priest is authorized to represent the whole Church at this gathering and to speak in the name of the whole Church and thus in the name of Christ himself. The priest acts in the name of Christ, the Head of the Church.

83 *Do all those present celebrate the Eucharist with the priest?*

All those present do celebrate the Eucharist in unity with the priest. They express this by taking part in the prayers and hymns, by listening to the Scripture readings and homily, and, above all, by sharing in the body and blood of Christ in Communion.

84 *How is Christ present in the Eucharist?*

Christ is present in the Eucharist in the hearts of those celebrating through grace, in the word of God that is proclaimed and preached, and, sacramentally, as priest in the actions of his minister, and as the food and drink that we share.

85 *When should we receive Communion?*

We should receive Communion whenever we are at Mass, provided that we are not conscious of being at enmity with God and our neighbor through grave sin.

Baptism

86 *What is Baptism?*

Baptism is the first sacrament of initiation into the Church. We are immersed or washed in water while the following words are spoken: "I baptize you in the name of the Father, and of the Son, and of the Holy Spirit."

87 *What mystery of the Church is signified and brought about in Baptism?*

The mystery of the Church signified and brought about in Baptism is our sacramental sharing in the priesthood of Christ by a permanent consecration to the Christian worship of God; this is called our baptismal character.

88 *How do we exercise our baptismal priesthood?*

We exercise our baptismal priesthood by acting as

Christ did in bringing humankind before God in our prayer and bringing God before humankind by our witness. We exercise this priestly ministry in the whole of our Christian lives, but especially when we minister to others in need. Although we may sometimes express it in ecclesial acts (as when we fulfill the office of reader, acolyte etc.), it is distinct from the sacramental ministry of the ordained priest (cf. q. 97ff.) in that it is not specifically directed to the ordering of the Church (cf. *Lumen Gentium*, 10, 11).

89 *Should Baptism ever be repeated?*

Baptism should never be repeated because our baptismal consecration is permanent.[4]

90 *What mystery of grace is signified and brought about in Baptism?*

The mystery of grace that is signified and brought about in Baptism is sanctifying grace, our sharing through faith in the life of the Spirit.

91 *In Baptism, are our sins forgiven?*

In Baptism, we are not only freed from slavery to original sin but, because we are sacramentally reborn and incorporated into Christ to live by his Spirit, all our past personal sins are forgiven as well.

92 *Is it appropriate to baptize babies?*

It is appropriate to baptize babies unless they are to be brought up in infidelity; for, being human, they are not to be deprived of the gift of the Spirit through faith, even though they are not yet capable of the beliefs in which this faith will be expressed.[5]

93 *When is Baptism to be celebrated?*

Baptism is most appropriately celebrated by the presiding bishop or priest during the Easter Vigil or at Pentecost or, failing that, in the course of a parish Mass; but it may be celebrated at any time and, in case of necessity, by anyone at all.

Confirmation

94 *What is Confirmation?*

Confirmation is the completion of Christian initiation into the Eucharistic life. It is normally celebrated by a bishop who anoints the recipient with chrism and says: "Be sealed with the Gift of the Holy Spirit." A priest may celebrate this sacrament when receiving a convert to full communion with the Church and on certain other occasions.

95 *What mystery of the Church is signified and brought about in Confirmation?*

The mystery of the Church that is signified and brought about in Confirmation is a sharing in the priesthood of Christ by a permanent consecration to the mission of Christian witness; this is called the character of Confirmation.

96 *What mystery of grace is signified and brought about in this sacrament?*

The mystery of grace that is signified and brought about in Confirmation is the indwelling of the Holy Spirit by which we are brought to maturity in Christ. We receive the gifts of "wisdom and understanding, of right judgment and courage, the gifts of knowledge and reverence, and the gift of wonder and awe in the presence of God" (cf. Is 11:2)[6] so that our lives become a witness to God's love.

Holy Orders

97 *What is the sacrament of Holy Orders?*

By the sacrament of Holy Orders particular men of the community are ordained to share in a special (sacramental) way in the priesthood of the Church, which is the priesthood of Christ. Their function is to represent Christ as well as to represent the Church, to offer worship, to teach and to govern the Christian community. Their priesthood, though related to the common priesthood of the baptized, is distinct from it in being directed specifically to the ordering of the Church (cf. *Lumen Gentium*, 10).

98 *What are the sacramental ministries in the Church?*

The sacramental ministries in the Church are those of bishop, priest, and deacon.

99 *What is a bishop?*

A bishop is a successor of the apostles with the responsibility for preaching the word of God, celebrating the sacraments, and governing the Church of a particular area.

100 *What is collegiality?*

Collegiality is the common responsibility which the bishops share for the entire Christian community throughout the world (cf. *Lumen Gentium*, 22).

101 *What is an ecumenical council?*

An ecumenical council is an exercise of collegiality in which the bishops of the world gather to promote the renewal of the Church and to decide questions of teaching and of Church order.

102 *What is the Pope?*

The Pope is the bishop of Rome and Patriarch of the Western Church. Because Rome is the traditional See of Peter, the leader of the apostles, its bishop has a primacy among all the bishops of the world and has a unique responsibility for the whole Church throughout the world.

103 *What is a priest of the Church?*

A priest is one appointed to cooperate with the bishop in the work of preaching and celebrating the sacraments (*Presbyterorum Ordinis*, 7).

104 *What is a deacon?*

A deacon is one appointed to cooperate with the bishop and priests in preaching, in the liturgy, and in organizing the almsgiving and social work of the Church (*Lumen Gentium*, 29).

105 *Who ordains bishops, priests, and deacons?*

Bishops, priests, and deacons are ordained by bishops with the consent of the people of God.

106 *What mystery of the Church is signified and brought about in the sacrament of Holy Orders?*

The mystery of the Church signified and brought about in this sacrament is ministerial character, a particular sharing in the priesthood of Christ by a permanent consecration to the work of the ministry.

107 *What mystery of grace is signified and brought about in the sacrament of Holy Orders?*

The mystery of grace signified and brought about in this sacrament is that indwelling of the Spirit by which ministers become not only officials of the Church, but in their lives also visible representatives of Christ carrying out their mission to preach the Gospel.

108 *What do we mean when we say that the Church is infallible?*

When we say that the Church is infallible we mean that when speaking as and for the whole Church, because of the guidance of the Holy Spirit, she cannot teach what is contrary to the Gospel; that is, on matters of faith or of morals she cannot be in error.

109 *How is the infallibility of the Church expressed?*

The infallibility of the Church is ordinarily expressed in the common teaching of her bishops and other preachers; on special occasions when an ecumenical council has to decide whether some disputed point of doctrine is the common teaching or not; and, occasionally, by the Pope making a similar decision outside a council but in consultation with the other bishops. Infallible decisions of this kind are extremely rare (cf. *Lumen Gentium*, 25).

Marriage

110 *What is the sacrament of Marriage?*

Marriage is the sacrament in which a baptized man and woman vow to belong to each other in a permanent, exclusive, sexual partnership of loving mutual care, concern, and shared responsibility, in the hope of having children and bringing up a family.

111 *Who celebrates the sacrament of Marriage?*

The celebrants of the sacrament of Marriage are the bride and bridegroom. However, for a valid celebration of the sacrament by one of her members, the Church, nowadays, normally requires that a priest and two others be present as witnesses to the vows.

112 *What mystery of the Church is signified and brought about in the sacrament of Marriage?*

The mystery of the Church signified and brought

about in this sacrament is the marriage bond: that sharing in the priesthood of Christ by which the two spouses are permanently consecrated to each other and to their children.

113 *What mystery of grace is signified and brought about in the sacrament of Marriage?*

The mystery of grace that is signified and brought about in the sacrament of Marriage is a sharing in the Spirit by which the two spouses grow in mutual love and are enabled to face together the problems of married life and to make of their family an image of the Church united in charity. This sacrament is a sign of the union in love between Christ and his Bride, the Church (cf. Eph 5).

114 *Can marriage be repeated?*

Marriage cannot normally be repeated while both partners are alive; for their consecration to each other is permanent. A civil divorce does not dissolve the valid marriage of baptized persons.

115 *What is an annulment?*

An annulment is an official recognition by the Church that what was thought to have been a marriage was, for one reason or another, invalid.

Penance (Reconciliation)

116 *What is the sacrament of Penance?*

The sacrament of Penance is the rite by which, through the ministry of the Church, we are reconciled to God even when we have sinned gravely (or "mortally," see q. 210) after being liberated from original sin in Baptism.

117 *What is required for the forgiveness of sins in this sacrament?*

For the forgiveness of grave sin through the sacrament of Penance, it is necessary that we should be sorry for our sin, wish to be forgiven, and propose, by God's grace, not to sin again. It is usually necessary that we confess all our grave sins to a priest[7] who will give us the absolution of the Church. A symbolic "penance" will normally be imposed, which we perform as a sign of our contrition for past sins and of our renewed life in Christ.

118 *What are the usual words of absolution?*

When giving absolution, the priest normally says: "God, the Father of mercies, through the death and resurrection of his Son, has reconciled the world to himself and sent the Holy Spirit among us for the forgiveness of sins; through the ministry of the Church, may God give you pardon and peace, and I absolve you from your sins, in the name of the Father, and of the Son, and of the Holy Spirit."

119 *What mystery of the Church is signified and brought about in the sacrament of Penance?*

The mystery of the Church signified and brought about in this sacrament is reconciliation with our fellow Christians, and the restoration of the exercise of our baptismal priesthood, which has been impeded by our sin.

120 *What mystery of grace is signified and brought about in the sacrament of Penance?*

The mystery of grace signified and brought about in this sacrament is contrition, that total conversion from sin by which we are reconciled to God and live once more as his friends and children, by his Holy Spirit (cf. q. 188).

121 *Is the sacrament of Penance only for those in grave sin?*

The sacrament of Penance is principally intended for those in grave sin, but it may also be genuinely celebrated by those whose sins do not amount to enmity with God (cf. qq. 215, 217).

122 *Is individual confession of all grave sins necessary for the celebration of this sacrament?*

Individual confession of grave sins is necessary for the private celebration of the sacrament. On certain rare, extraordinary occasions, general absolution is given to many people at once. But even in these cases the penitents must have the intention of individually confessing their grave sins when the opportunity arises.

123 *Can grave sins be forgiven without the sacraments of Baptism or Penance?*

If the celebration of Baptism or Penance is prevented, grave sins can be forgiven through honest desire for these sacraments, without the actual celebration of either. But these sins must still be confessed when the person is able to do so.

124 *Can sins that are not grave be forgiven without the sacrament of Penance?*

Sins that are not grave are forgiven by any increase in our love for God and for each other. The forgiveness of such sins is part of the celebration of the sacrament of love, the Eucharist.

The Anointing of the Sick

125 *What is the Anointing of the Sick?*

The sacrament of the Anointing of the Sick is the rite in which one who is seriously ill is prayed for by the Church and anointed with oil as a sign of healing (cf. Jas 5:14–6).

126 *What mystery of the Church is signified and brought about in this sacrament?*

The mystery of the Church that is signified and brought about in the sacrament of Anointing is the strengthening of the sick so that they may either be restored to the public exercise of their baptismal priesthood, which has been impeded by sickness, or else make of their act of death a final sharing in the priestly act of Christ.

127 *What mystery of grace is signified and brought about in this sacrament?*

The mystery of grace signified and brought about in the sacrament of Anointing of the Sick is the renewal of the life of the Spirit so that the recipient, whether in recovery or in dying, may be united more closely with Christ our healer and be a sign of love to the world.

128 *By whom should this sacrament be received?*

This sacrament should be received by any of the baptized as soon as they are found to be suffering from serious sickness—the kind of sickness which might be given as a cause of death—or even if they are simply in danger of death from old age. If death seems imminent, this sacrament is accompanied by Viaticum, the last Communion before the journey through death to resurrection.

The Members of the Church

129 *Who are the members of the Church on earth?*

The members of the Church on earth are all those who, having been baptized, have not rejected belief in the Gospel as handed down in the Tradition of the Church.

130 *Is the Church only those living on earth?*

The Church includes not only those alive today but also all those who have died in friendship with God and await the resurrection. The saints in heaven join with us in our prayer and praise of the Father, through the Son, in the Holy Spirit.

131 *What is a saint?*

A saint is one who lives by the Holy Spirit, and in this sense all are called to be saints, but the word is also used to mean those especially holy men and women whom the Church (often by canonization) recommends to us as examples of virtue and holiness and whose public cult she permits.

132 *Is the Church only for holy people?*

The Church is not only for holy people but for sinners, for, in her, Jesus continues his compassion for his weak fellow human beings who are beset by temptations and surrounded by the forces of sin and death.

133 *Are all holy people members of the Church?*

Not all holy people are members of the Church in this world, for the gift of the Spirit is not confined to its visible, sacramental expression in the Church. All such holy people, however, receive the Spirit through the cross of Christ, which is preached and shown to us only in the Church.

134 *Why is the Church called the Church of the Poor?*

The Church is called the Church of the Poor because Christ said that the kingdom belongs to the poor, and the Church is dedicated to upholding the cause of the needy and the oppressed, and because Christ promised that the Church would be hated by those wealthy and powerful persons who are so preoccupied with this world as to exclude God and his law (cf. *Gaudium et Spes*, 1).

135 *What are monks, friars, and religious?*

They are groups of men and women who, out of love for God and all men and women, dedicate themselves by vow to serve the Gospel in a life of evangelical poverty as a community of celibates. They promise obedience in accordance with a rule approved by the Church, and usually celebrate communally and with solemnity the Divine Office and other liturgy.

Mary

136 *Who is the greatest of the saints?*

The greatest of the saints is Mary, the Virgin Mother of God, also called Our Lady. By accepting the motherhood of Jesus, she brought God's salvation to the world. When the angel told her that she was to be Mother of the Savior, she said: "Here I am, the servant of the Lord; let it be with me according to your word" (Lk 1:38).

137 *What is the most common prayer to Our Lady?*

The most common prayer to Our Lady is the Hail Mary:

> Hail Mary, full of grace, the Lord is with you; blessed are you among women and blessed is the fruit of your womb, Jesus. Holy Mary, Mother of God, pray for us sinners now and at the hour of our death. Amen (cf. Lk 1:28, 42; and cf. q. 180).

138 *What is the doctrine of the Immaculate Conception?*

The doctrine of the Immaculate Conception is that in Mary our liberation from sin is anticipated; for, through the foreseen merits of her Son, she was redeemed by being preserved from that original sin in which the rest of the redeemed were conceived.

139 *What is the doctrine of the Assumption?*

The doctrine of the Assumption is that in Mary our liberation from death, our resurrection, is anticipated; for her redemption is such that, like her Son, she is already humanly alive in heaven, body and soul.

140 *Why do we especially pray to Mary?*

We especially pray to Mary, the Mother of God, because Jesus on the cross gave her to us as our

Mother; for she is the type or image of our mother the Church, and she shows us, in her life, what God does for those he loves and redeems.

The Institutions of the Church

141 *How is the Church organized?*

The Church consists of sees or dioceses, local churches governed by their bishops. These bishops are in communion with each other and with the Church of Rome, whose bishop is the Pope.

142 *Are all these local churches the same?*

These local churches may differ in many ways in their liturgy and in their particular traditions, but they share common Scriptures, a common faith, and common sacraments.

143 *What are, today, the main groups of churches?*

The main groups of Churches are the ancient Churches of the Eastern Rites and the Church of the Western (Latin) Rite. Because of historical conflicts, many churches of Eastern Rites are not, at present, in full communion with Rome and do not accept the primacy of the bishop of Rome, although they share the same Scripture, faith, and sacraments; these are called the Orthodox Churches. The Western Church itself was divided at the time of the Reformation, and there are many Christian churches and ecclesial communities that do not accept the whole Tradition of Scripture, faith, and sacraments in the forms handed down by the Churches in communion with Rome. These churches are usually known as the Reformed or Protestant churches.

144 *What is ecumenism?*

Ecumenism is the movement within the Christian churches to respond to the Prayer of Christ (Jn 17) so that, in a spirit of repentance for our divisions, we may be led by the Holy Spirit to achieve full communion in organic unity.

145 *What rules has the Western Church made for her members?*

Besides some minor regulations, the main rules governing members of the Western Church oblige them to attend Mass on Sundays and certain major feasts (known as holy days of obligation); to follow the local regulations concerning penance on Ash Wednesday, Good Friday, and other Fridays; to celebrate the sacrament of Penance once a year if they have committed grave sin, and to receive Communion during the Easter season; to contribute financially to the upkeep of the Church and its almsgiving; and not to marry within certain degrees of kindred.

146 *What are the holy days of obligation in the United States and Canada?*

In the United States

January 1:	The Solemnity of Mary, Mother of God
	Ascension of Our Lord *(40 days after Easter)*
August 15:	The Assumption of the Blessed Virgin Mary
November 1:	All Saints' Day
December 8:	The Immaculate Conception
December 25:	Christmas Day*

In Canada

January 1:	The Solemnity of Mary, Mother of God
December 25:	Christmas Day

---

* *Note:* Christmas is always a holy day of obligation on whatever day it falls. When the feasts of the Assumption, All Saints, or the Solemnity of Mary, Mother of God (January 1) are celebrated on a Saturday or Monday, there is no obligation to participate in Mass. The Immaculate Conception remains a holy day of obligation except when December 8 falls on Sunday. Then the feast is transferred to Monday, in which case it is not considered a holy day. However, the faithful are still encouraged to participate at Mass on these days.

In many dioceses, the feast of the Ascension is transferred to the seventh Sunday of Easter.

147 *What is the Church with its institutions for?*

The Church exists to proclaim the coming of the kingdom of God and to foster in us that life in the Spirit by which the kingdom is already beginning.

Part Three

Life in the Spirit

Virtues

148 *What is a virtue?*

A virtue is a settled disposition, acquired by practice or given as a grace, to behave in ways appropriate to the good life.

149 *What is the good life?*

The good life is life in friendship with God and with other people, in and through which we come to happiness.

150 *What are the principal virtues directly bearing on our friendship with God?*

The principal virtues directly bearing on our friendship with God are called the theological virtues: they are faith, hope, and charity.

151 *What are the other principal virtues?*

The other principal virtues, which bear on our friendship with God through our friendship with other people, are called the cardinal virtues: they are justice, courage, temperateness, and good sense (prudence).

152 *Can we acquire the cardinal virtues by our own efforts and through education?*

By our own efforts and through education we can acquire an incomplete form of the cardinal virtues, which dispose us to live well in secular society. But because this society is itself for the sake of the kingdom of God, the cardinal virtues need to be perfected and enlivened by the theological virtues, especially charity.

153 *Can we acquire the theological virtues by our own efforts?*

We cannot acquire the theological virtues by our own efforts. They are a gift from God that surpasses anything within human power.

Faith

154 *What is faith?*

Faith is a divinely given disposition of the mind, by which we begin to share in God's understanding of himself. In faith, we think of the history of humanity and our own life story as centered on the love of God for us as revealed in the Son of God, Jesus Christ, the Word of God made flesh.

155 *What is God's understanding of himself?*

God's understanding of himself is the Father's eternal speaking of the Word (which is the Father's begetting of the Son).

156 *What beliefs does faith entail?*

Faith is belief, first of all, in God himself. For those to whom the Gospel has been preached, it entails believing all that is revealed by God, simply because it is the word of God, handed down to us in Christ's Church through the tradition of the Scriptures.

157 *Where are we to find the principal mysteries of the faith proposed for our belief?*

We are to find the principal mysteries of the faith proposed for our belief in the creeds of the Church.

158 *What is the Apostles' Creed?*

The Apostles' Creed is a very early formulation of the Tradition of the Church. It states:

> I believe in God, the Father almighty, creator of heaven and earth. I believe in Jesus Christ, his only Son, our Lord. He was conceived by

> the power of the Holy Spirit and born of the Virgin Mary. He suffered under Pontius Pilate, was crucified, died, and was buried. He descended to the dead. On the third day he rose again. He ascended into heaven and is seated at the right hand of the Father. He will come again to judge the living and the dead. I believe in the Holy Spirit, the holy Catholic Church, the communion of saints, the forgiveness of sins, the resurrection of the body, and life everlasting. Amen.

159 *Are we saved by faith?*

We are saved by a living faith, which is the free gift of God. We cannot deserve it by any works or merits of our own.

160 *To whom has God given the free gift of living faith?*

God offers the gift of living faith in different ways to everyone, for he "desires all to be saved and to come to the knowledge of the truth" (I Tim 2:4). But it is possible for us to make no use of his gift and even to lose it (cf. Mt 25:14–30).

161 *What is the minimum of belief by which any adult will normally express the faith he has been offered?*

The belief that God exists and cares for us. For "whoever would draw near to God must believe that he exists and that he rewards those who seek him" (Heb 11:6).

162 *Have all atheists rejected the gift of faith?*

Not all who are called atheists have necessarily rejected the gift of faith; they may merely reject some particular image or understanding of the mystery of God. In such matters, only God himself can know our hearts with any certainty.

163 *How is God's giving of faith visible to us?*

God's giving of faith to humankind is visible in the Church and especially in the sacrament of Baptism, but God also works in ways that are unknown to us.

164 *What is it to have dead faith?*

To have dead faith is to believe in what God has revealed but not to center our lives upon it. It is faith deprived of its completion in charity, and it does not save us.

165 *How are we principally to cultivate the virtue of faith?*

We are to practice and cultivate our faith first of all by prayer to our Father, the giver of faith, to make our faith stronger and more mature. We should pray: "Lord, I believe; help my unbelief" (Mk 9:24).

166 *In what other ways are we to practice and cultivate our faith?*

We also practice and cultivate our faith by reflection on the mysteries that have been revealed and their relevance to our lives, especially by listening to the readings from Scripture during Mass or reading Scripture ourselves, whether in study groups or privately, and by taking advantage of whatever means are available to us to deepen our understanding of the Gospel.

167 *Is it an exercise of faith to try to understand the arguments of those who reject the Gospel and the Church?*

An honest and informed examination of such arguments may be an exercise of the virtue of faith, for it may deepen our understanding, enable us to distinguish the Gospel itself from our prejudices, and bring us to better ways of formulating our belief. We need not be afraid of encountering any cogent arguments against the Gospel because what is proposed for our belief is true. However, we first need to be well-grounded in our faith before attempting this.

168 *How can we fail in the exercise of the virtue of faith?*

We fail totally in the exercise of faith if we clearly and consciously reject the tradition of God's revelation, but we also fail to some degree if we do not frequently reflect on what God has done for us in Christ, if we neglect opportunities for finding out more about the Gospel, and if we fail to explain our belief to those who seriously inquire of us.

169 *Is it a failure in faith to be unable to see how some part of the creed could be true?*

It is not a failure in faith to be unable to see how some part of the creed could be true, but in such a case, we are to ask the help of God in prayer and the help of the Church by consulting others who may understand our difficulties and be able to help us to resolve them.

Hope

170 *What is hope?*

Hope is a divinely given disposition by which we respond to and cooperate with God's providence: by hope, we are confident that God plans to bring humankind to the kingdom in Christ, and that only by unrepented grave sin can we exclude ourselves from it.

171 *What is the principal expression of the virtue of hope?*

The principal expression of the virtue of hope is our prayer.

172 *What is the first prayer?*

The first prayer is the sacrifice of Christ, by which, in his love for and obedience to the Father, he accepted death on the cross as a prayer for our salvation and for the coming of the kingdom. All our prayers are ways of sharing in that communication between the Son and the Father.

173 *How do we share in Christ's prayer to the Father?*

We share in Christ's prayer principally in the Eucharist—which is the sacrament of the cross—in the other sacraments, and, in general, in the liturgical prayer of the whole Church as well as in our personal prayers.

174 *How did Jesus teach his disciples to pray?*

Jesus said: "When you are praying, do not heap up empty phrases as the Gentiles do; for they think that they will be heard because of their many words. Do not be like them, for your Father knows what you need before you ask him. Pray then in this way:

> "Our Father, who art in heaven, hallowed be
> thy name;
> thy kingdom come; thy will be done on earth as
> it is in heaven.
> Give us this day our daily bread;
> and forgive us our trespasses
> as we forgive those who trespass against us;
> and lead us not into temptation, but deliver us
> from evil" (Mt 6:7–13).

175 *Should we pray for our personal wants in prayer of petition?*

We should pray for our personal wants and needs, for in doing so we acknowledge God as our Father and friend who cares for us in the details of our lives.

176 *Do we pray in the hope of changing God's mind?*

By prayer we do not hope to change God's mind, for we know him to be eternally unchanging and constantly loving. But he wills from eternity that we should receive his gifts in answer to our prayer; for it is he who gives us the grace to pray (cf. "Our desire to thank you is itself your gift," Weekday Preface IV).

177 *Did Jesus give us an example of prayer of petition?*

Jesus gave us an example of prayer of petition when he said: "My Father, if it is possible, let this cup pass from me; yet not what I want but what you want" (Mt 26:39).

178 *Is prayer always answered?*

Prayer is always answered in the sense that no prayer goes unheard. But instead of giving us what we ask, God may give us something greater that we need more deeply.

179 *Is there other prayer besides the prayer of petition?*

Besides the prayer of petition, there is also prayer of thanksgiving and of praise. Meditation, or reflection on the mysteries of faith, is closely related to prayer and will naturally lead to it. A popular form of this is the Rosary.

180 *Should we pray only to God?*

We should pray only to God. We normally pray to the Father, through the Son, in the Holy Spirit. But we may pray to the saints in heaven, especially Mary, the Mother of God, in the sense of asking them to pray to God with us and for us, just as we ask our fellow Christians on earth to pray for us.

181 *Should we pray with the Christians of separated churches?*

We should pray with the Christians of separated churches as the surest way of healing the divisions of the Church. We should pray, too, with non-Christians, unless these prayers are likely to give rise to misunderstanding of our belief. (In such a case, it is normally the responsibility of the bishop to decide what is appropriate to do.)

182 *What is liturgy?*

The liturgy is the official public prayer of the Church. It consists in the celebration of the Eucharist and other sacraments, together with the Divine Office and certain other ceremonies.

183 *What is the Divine Office?*

The Divine Office is a communal daily prayer consisting of the singing or reciting of psalms and hymns, with readings from Scripture and other Christian writings.

184 *What is the liturgical year?*

The liturgical year is the distribution of the liturgy throughout the year. Essentially, it consists in the season of Easter (from Easter to Pentecost and preceded by the penitential season of Lent, starting on Ash Wednesday), in which we celebrate the resurrection of Christ from the dead; and the season of Advent through Christmas to Epiphany, in which we celebrate his incarnation, and look forward to his coming again in glory. The rest of the year is known as "ordinary time." There is also a concurrent cycle of feasts of saints.

185 *What is the last week in Lent called?*

The last week in Lent, an immediate preparation for Easter, is called Holy Week. Its last three days: Holy Thursday, Good Friday, and Holy Saturday, constitute a solemn commemoration of the passion and death of Christ.

186 *How should we celebrate Lent?*

We should celebrate Lent as a preparation for Easter by intensifying our life of prayer, by almsgiving, and by adopting some penitential discipline such as fasting.

187 *How should we celebrate Easter?*

We should celebrate Easter with praise and rejoicing in gratitude for the resurrection, and, if possible, we should attend the Easter Vigil on the night of Holy Saturday, renew our baptismal vows, and share in the Eucharist.

188 *How, besides in our prayer, do we exercise the virtue of hope?*

Contrition, the recognition that I am a sinner whom God loves, forgives, and is transforming into a saint, is an expression of hope. It is wholly different from an anxious sense of guilt. It is also an exercise of hope to recognize that God's love will transform our sinful world, and that, whatever setbacks we may experience, we can be confident that our struggle for a more just and peaceful society is working to fulfill the plan of God's providence and that what we strive for will be achieved in the future coming of the kingdom of God.

189 *How can we fail in the virtue of hope?*

We can fail in the virtue of hope by neglecting our part in the sacraments and other prayers of the Church, by failing to ask God for the grace we need to remain in his friendship, and by losing heart in our struggle against the powers of this world.

190 *What attitudes are especially contrary to the virtue of hope?*

Two opposing attitudes are especially contrary to the virtue of hope: despair and presumption.

191 *What is despair?*

Despair is the deliberately encouraged choice to believe that, because of the power of sin, God's love is not sufficient to save me or to transform the world. Despair says: It is useless to pray for God's grace or to work for his kingdom.

192 *What is presumption?*

Presumption is the deliberately encouraged choice to believe that, because there is enough goodness in myself and in the world, God will automatically save me and will transform the world without my struggle. Presumption says: It is needless to pray for God's grace or to work for justice and peace.

193 *What do despair and presumption have in common?*

They both involve an estimate of myself and my world rather than confidence in God's love.

Charity

194 *What is charity?*

Charity is the divinely given disposition of the will by which we are friends with God. By charity God enables us to love him in friendship, to share in his enjoyment of the divine life, and to love others as he loves them.

195 *What is God's enjoyment of the divine life?*

God's enjoyment of the divine life is the Holy Spirit.

196 *What are friends?*

Friends are attracted to each other, accept each other, seek each other's good, and share the enjoyment of a common life.

197 *How do we share a common life with God?*

We share a common life with God by receiving the Holy Spirit, who dwells in us, along with the gift of sanctifying grace.

198 *Does charity belong only to the life of this world?*

No. Unlike faith, hope, and the sacraments of the Church, charity does not belong to this life only but is the friendship that constitutes the kingdom.

199 *What is the principal exercise of charity?*

The principal exercise of charity is love, which is to wish someone well and to desire to be united with her or him.

200 *Is there an order of priority in charity?*

There is an order of priority in charity: we should love God first, then ourselves, then our neighbor, and finally our bodily life.

201 *What is it to love God?*

To love God is to seek union with him more than any other good and to reject sin by which we separate ourselves from him.

202 *What is it to love ourselves?*

To love ourselves is to seek our greatest good, which is the fulfillment and happiness of the kingdom, already present as charity during this life.

203 *What is it to love our neighbors?*

To love our neighbors is to seek their good when that is possible and never to seek their ultimate harm, because they are fellow members of human society, but more fundamentally because they are beloved of God and made, like us, for the kingdom—brothers and sisters "for whom Christ died" (Rom 14:15).

204 *What is it to love my bodily life?*

To love my bodily life is to cherish and preserve my life, to delight in the health and activity of my body, and to respect it as the body in which I communicate with others and in which I will be raised from the dead to live eternally in the kingdom. For "your body is a temple of the Holy Spirit" (1 Cor 6:19).

205 *Who is my neighbor?*

All human beings are my neighbors and I must love them all. But it is reasonable and natural that I should love those closest to me (my family, my fellow workers, fellow citizens, and fellow Christians) more than others, and especially more than my enemies.

206 *Can we wish harm to our enemies?*

We can wish sufficient harm to our enemies to restrain their injustice, and we may wish that criminals should be justly punished to protect the common good, but we must still wish them, as God does, to be united with us in the kingdom.

207 *What of those who harm us without being unjust?*

Those who harm us justly are not our enemies, but they act as friends through whom God is correcting us and bringing us closer to himself.

208 *How do we usually exercise charity toward others?*

We usually exercise charity toward others by seeking their good and supplying their needs; by readily forgiving their offenses; by mercy; by thinking and speaking of their good points; by helping them in temptation, sickness, ignorance, or poverty; by seeking to enjoy their company.

209 *Is almsgiving a special act of charity?*

Almsgiving is a special act of charity, but a greater one is to struggle for a more just society in which almsgiving will be less necessary.

210 *What do we call an act that is directly destructive of charity?*

An act directly contrary to charity is called mortal (or deadly) sin, because it destroys the friendship that is the life of God in us.

211 *After committing mortal sin, can we restore this life by our own efforts?*

After committing mortal sin, we cannot of ourselves even begin to desire the restoration of our divine life, just as we could not rise from the dead by our own efforts. But by the prompting of God's grace, we may seek his mercy and forgiveness, which is always available to those who call on him.

212 *What kind of actions are mortal sins?*

Mortal sins are the kind of sins directly forbidden by the Ten Commandments, for these lay down the minimal conditions for friendship with God and each other: sins such as the deliberate rejection of God, murder, rape, adultery, perjury, oppression of the poor, and the like.

213 *Can there be mitigating circumstances in which a person doing such an action would not commit a mortal sin?*

There can be mitigating circumstances such as honest ignorance or lack of true consent. The act itself, however, remains opposed to our true good and still has harmful effects. That is why it is very important to have a correctly formed conscience.

214 *Is ignorance always an excuse?*

Ignorance is not always an excuse, for some ignorance can only be due to irresponsibility or self-deception.

215 *What are venial sins?*

Venial sins are faults that are not sinful in the same sense as mortal sins. They do not destroy or even diminish the life of charity, but they are failures in the exercise of virtue so that we are less Christlike than we could be. They attach us to the things of this world and, in time, lay us open to temptations to mortal sin.

216 *What are we to do if we commit mortal sin?*

If we commit mortal sin we must repent and seek reconciliation with God and the Church in the sacrament of Penance. If the sacrament is not available, we must pray for the grace of the sacrament, which is true contrition by which we are converted to the life of the Spirit.

217 *What are we to do when we have committed venial sins?*

When we have committed venial sins, we must actively seek occasions for practicing charity in loving acts (especially rather difficult ones that will help us to discipline ourselves), and strengthen our union with

God and the Church through prayer and in particular through joining in the Eucharistic meal. We may also confess some of our venial sins in the sacrament of Penance.

218 *How do we fail in the exercise of charity toward others?*

We fail totally in the exercise of charity by any mortal sin, by which we reject God's friendship. We may fail in charity toward others by indifference or hostility toward them; by being slow to forgive; by bearing grudges; by envy, jealousy, and spitefulness; by acting harshly or violently; by thinking ill or speaking ill of others (especially when it is false); by neglecting them in their needs.

Justice

219 *What is justice?*

Justice is a disposition of the will that inclines us to give to every person what is her or his due with a view to the common good of the whole society.

220 *How do we exercise the virtue of justice?*

We exercise the virtue of justice by obeying the law and upholding the common good in a just society; by seeking to change an unjust society; by concern for the rights of others in their reputation, dignity, and property; by speaking truthfully and dealing honestly with our neighbor.

221 *What is an unjust society?*

An unjust society is one in which some section of the community is systematically exploited in the interests of another wealthy and powerful section. Although we must use every means in our power to liberate such a society, we know that, because of original sin, any society will be unjust in some respects until the coming of the kingdom.

222 *Is it an exercise of the virtue of justice to work for peace?*

It is an important exercise of the virtue of justice to work for peace, for the enemy of peace is always injustice.

223 *Can it be an exercise of justice to struggle against my neighbor?*

It is an exercise of justice to struggle to restrain an injustice that my neighbor may commit, support, or condone, provided that in doing so I do not myself act unjustly.

224 *Can war or violent struggle ever be just?*

War or violent struggle can never be just except in very special circumstances: that it is the only way of restraining a very great injustice, that it will not itself bring about greater destruction than the evil it opposes, that it has a reasonable chance of success, that it does not involve acts of injustice such as the deliberate killing of non-combatants, and that those who wage it are authorized to do so by a large degree of popular support.

225 *Is the use of weapons of mass destruction ever just?*

The use of weapons of mass destruction, such as nuclear missiles, is never just, for it involves the wholesale murder of non-combatants.[8]

226 *Can I be unjust to myself?*

I cannot, strictly speaking, be unjust to myself as I can to another individual, but some kinds of self-injury detract from what is demanded by the common good of society. Thus suicide, self-mutilation (including sterilization), and even serious failure to use and develop my talents may be contrary to justice.

227 *Is all justice social justice?*

Not all justice is social justice. There is also justice in the family or religious community and in the Church.

228 *How is justice exercised in the family?*

Justice is exercised in the family by a practical concern for the equality of husband and wife, and by providing for the dignity of children and their needs with respect to health and education.

229 *How is justice exercised in a religious community?*

Justice is exercised in a religious community by careful observance of the rule and constitution, so that superiors do not exceed their authority and the rights of all members are properly respected. Justice also demands that religious do not use the respect in which they are commonly held to exploit others, especially their employees.

230 *How is justice exercised in the Church?*

Justice is exercised in the Church by practical concern for those groups which may not yet have sufficient official voice in the Church, notably the laity and women; by the efficient and speedy dispatch of legal justice, especially in marriage cases; and by respect for legitimate freedom of opinion within the Church.

231 *How can we fail in the exercise of justice?*

We fail in the exercise of justice by depriving others of their due or failing to defend them against injustice: by murder, abortion, injury—including self-injury, torture, rape, and adultery; by collusion with an oppressive and exploitative regime or with an unjust war; by indulging racism, sexism, or religious bigotry; by avarice, by accumulating wealth and keeping it from the poor; by stealing or misusing the legitimate property of the community or individuals; by tax evasion and inequitable forms of legal tax avoidance; by spreading deceptive propaganda or misleading advertising; by perjury and all forms of dishonest or sharp practice; and by any form of cooperation with the injustice of others.

232 *Should all acts of injustice be forbidden by the law of the land?*

Not all unjust or otherwise sinful acts should be forbidden by law, for the law is concerned with the protection and promotion of the common good of society. While all sinful acts, however "private," damage the common good, in many cases to make them illegal would do even more damage. In such matters legislators must exercise the virtue of good sense.

233 *What must we do if we have committed a sin of injustice?*

When we have committed a sin of injustice, we must seek the forgiveness of God and of those we have wronged, and we must work to restore the damage we have done to them.

Courage

234 *What is courage?*

Courage is a disposition of our feelings of aggression that inclines us, characteristically, to face up to and deal with difficulties and dangers for the sake of doing what is good. A courageous person is neither overaggressive nor timid, is angry about the right things at the right time, and is prepared to suffer patiently when it is necessary and even to die for the sake of justice or in witness to the Gospel. Such a person does not need to make an effort of will to behave well in the face of difficulties to be overcome.

235 *How do we exercise the virtue of courage?*

We exercise the virtue of courage principally in energetic struggle on behalf of the poor and the weak, and on every occasion when we have to face hostility and danger for the sake of justice and the Gospel.

236 *What do we call one who dies in witness to the Gospel?*

One who accepts death in witness to the Gospel is called a martyr.

237 *How do we fail in the exercise of courage?*

We fail in the exercise of courage by acquiescence in injustice through fear of the powerful or of public opinion, by conformity with the values of this world, and by all forms of cowardice and laziness, by unreasonable anger and bad temper, and by irresponsible rashness.

Temperateness

238 *What is temperateness?*

Temperateness is a disposition of our sensual desires that inclines us, characteristically, to behave well in the face of what is pleasurable and attractive. Temperate people are neither cold and inhibited, nor greedy and self-indulgent. It is relatively rare for them to have to restrain their desires by an effort of will.

239 *In what areas is this virtue most commonly exercised?*

Temperateness is primarily exercised in respect of our attitude to our own pleasure in eating and in sex. It is secondarily exercised in respect of our attitude to the suffering of others[9]—thus it includes such dispositions as gentleness and compassion. We fail in it by callousness and by all delight in violence and cruelty.

240 *How do we exercise temperateness in the matter of eating and drinking?*

We exercise the virtue of temperateness in the matter of eating and drinking by, characteristically, taking and enjoying what is sufficient for our health and for the entertainment of our friends.

241 *How do we fail in the exercise of temperateness in this area?*

We may fail by indifference to the enjoyments of the table, by eating and drinking that is totally divorced from either friendship or the requirements of health, by eating what is merely superficially attractive at the expense of a reasonable diet, by drug abuse, and by all forms of gluttony and drunkenness.

242 *What do we call temperateness in the matter of sex?*

The virtue of temperateness in the matter of sex is called chastity.

243 *How do we exercise chastity?*

We exercise the virtue of chastity by, characteristically, being warm and affectionate but not flirtatious with others, by ensuring that embraces and other bodily gestures are genuinely signs of friendship, and having genital sex only with the one to whom we are exclusively committed in marriage.

244 *How do we exercise the virtue of chastity in marriage?*

We exercise the virtue of chastity in marriage by frequent expression of our love, especially through mutually desired sexual intercourse, in the hope of having a reasonable number of children at appropriate times.

245 *Does a chaste person only have sexual relations with a view to having children?*

A chaste person does not have sexual relations only with a view to having children, for sex is also an expression of and constituent of marital friendship and may be celebrated even when conception is known to be impossible. If natural family planning is used at certain times to avoid conception, however, it cannot be used permanently to avoid having any children at all.

246 *What does the Catholic Church teach about the use of birth control?*

It teaches that it is right and proper for parents to regulate the number of children they have and to space them out in the family, but not by means which artificially make it impossible for sexual intercourse to result in conception. When husband and wife unite so as to become "one flesh," their mutual self-gift bespeaks a total love that does not hold back anything of themselves, including their fertility. Contraception contradicts this language of the body.

247 *How can we fail in the exercise of chastity?*

We fail in the exercise of chastity by dislike or fear of sex, and by all sex that is wholly without friendship or from which any connection with raising a family is deliberately excluded, that is, by all sexual acts outside of marriage: by masturbation, by sex simply for individual gratification without concern for the other partner, by rape, adultery, and promiscuity, by intercourse with a partner of the same sex, by intercourse with a member of another species, by self-indulgent sexual fantasies and the use of pornography to procure such fantasies.

Good Sense (Prudence)

248 *What is good sense?*

Good sense (or prudence) is a disposition of the mind by which we readily understand how, in practice, to apply general moral principles in particular cases and thus to exercise all our virtues intelligently and effectively.

249 *In what areas do we principally exercise the virtue of good sense?*

We exercise good sense with regard to management of our affairs, and thus principally in the life of the whole society, in the life of the family or religious community, and in our private lives.

250 *How do we exercise good sense with respect to the whole society?*

We exercise good sense with respect to the whole society by taking an interest in politics and current affairs and interpreting public life in terms of justice and charity, so that our exercise of power will be reasoned and in accordance with the Gospel rather than merely an act of self-interest or unthinking habit.

251 *How do we exercise the virtue of good sense in the family or community?*

We exercise good sense with respect to the domestic community by seeking to understand its practical needs: by insuring that there is communication and consultation about them and about what is to be done, and by instituting a domestic life that is neither extravagant nor miserly.

252 *How do we exercise good sense with respect to our personal lives?*

We exercise good sense in our personal lives by thinking carefully before we make important decisions and by placing our actions in the context of some honest attempt to know ourselves as we are, by consulting with others when we are in doubt about what is to be done, and, in general, by acting in particular cases with consideration for our own good and happiness and for that of others.

253 *How can we fail in the exercise of good sense?*

We fail in good sense by the exercise of cunning to encompass bad ends as well as by foolishness while trying to do good; by all forms of unreasonableness, self-deception, bigotry, and prejudice; by pedantic legalism; by being doctrinaire; by voting ignorantly, irresponsibly, or merely selfishly; by careless incompetence in the management of domestic affairs; and by leading a life without any conscious purpose or meaning.

The Last Things

254 *What is death?*

Death is the completion of life in this world. By the power of the Spirit we accept it as Christ did, and come through it with him to eternal life.

255 *When do we sacramentally accept death with Christ?*

We sacramentally accept death with Christ in Baptism. "We were buried with him by Baptism into death, so that as Christ was raised from the dead by the glory of the Father, we too might walk in newness of life" (Rom 6:4).

256 *In what other ways do we accept death in Christ?*

In our daily lives we accept death in Christ whenever, by the power of the Spirit, we take up our cross and follow him by denying ourselves and giving ourselves in love to others.

257 *Can we accept death if we die rejecting God's offer of love and mercy?*

If we die rejecting God's gift of the Spirit, we are unable to accept death, so that it remains our enemy for ever. This is called hell.

258 *Is death terrible?*

Even though by the power of the Spirit we accept death in Christ, it is still terrible, for by death, we are stripped of all that attached us to the things of this world. It is the more terrible the more we have allowed ourselves to be attached to them.

259 *How do we become attached to the things of this world?*

We become more attached to the things of this world whenever we fail in love by any kind of sin, and this attachment may remain even after our sin is forgiven.

260 *How do we become detached from the things of this world so that we may be prepared for death?*

We become detached from the things of this world by penance and mortification, especially by almsgiving and all forms of difficult work for others in need.

261 *What do we call the detachment from things of this world that remains for us in death?*

The final detachment from the things of this world that happens to us when we die in Christ is called purgatory.

262 *Do we die alone?*

We do not die alone, unless we reject God's love and mercy. We die in Christ, in the presence of God, and in the company of our fellow Christians. Our mother the Church stands with us in death as the Mother of Jesus stood by his cross. This is the meaning of Viaticum and the Church's prayers for the dead.

263 *Is it proper to grieve for the dead?*

It is proper to grieve for those who by death are separated from us more completely than by any other kind of bodily absence. But just as our sorrow for sin in contrition is not cancelled by but taken up into our confidence in God's mercy and forgiveness, so our grief for the dead is taken up into our sure hope of the resurrection.

264 *To what are we destined beyond death?*

All the faithful are destined beyond death to the resurrection, when the kingdom of God will be finally established and we shall live our own real bodily lives, transfigured by the Spirit and, in Christ, share the Father's eternal life of understanding and joy. This is called heaven.

Notes

1. God is conventionally referred to as "he" or "him," but this must not be understood as ascribing any gender to him.

2. *Christos* is the Greek equivalent of the Hebrew Messiah, meaning "the anointed one," implying one filled with the spirit or breath of God. This anointing was especially associated with kingship, and "Messiah" came to be used of the Savior King who was to come.

3. Cf. Eucharistic Prayer I: "May all of us who share in the body and blood of Christ [mystery of the Church] be brought together in unity by the Holy Spirit [mystery of grace]."

4. The permanence of the dedication or consecration, which is the mystery of the Church in this sacrament, belongs also to the sacraments of Confirmation and Holy Orders and, in its own way, to the sacrament of Marriage (cf. qq. 95, 106, 114).

5. What happens to those who die unbaptized? If they are adults capable of personal decision they may, in countless ways, desire the grace of the sacrament—even if they do not even know of the sacrament itself (cf. 74, 162). St. Augustine thought that unbaptized infants who died before being able to make such a personal choice could not enter heaven and must, therefore, be condemned to hell. St. Thomas Aquinas and others, opposing this grim view, postulated a destiny, "Limbo," which involved neither the suffering of hell nor the beatitude of heaven. Some mod-

ern theologians have argued, for various reasons, that such children simply go to heaven. The Church has not defined anything on this matter. We therefore do not know with certainty what is the fate of infants who die unbaptized. What we do know with certainty is that God loves each of them infinitely more than any of us could.

In April 2007, with the approval of Pope Benedict XVI, the International Theological Commission issued a document stating that we have firm reasons for hope that these infants will be saved.

6. These qualities of sensitivity to the promptings of the Spirit are traditionally known as the seven gifts of the Spirit.

7. "Why should I have to confess to a priest?" is a very common and natural question. Are the clergy, after all, simply setting themselves up as the channel (and therefore, perhaps, the barrier) between the sinner and the God of mercy? There are two things to consider: why the Church is involved and why the priest is involved.

It is certainly true that God's mercy and love may come to us alone in countless unknown ways. We may be given the grace of conversion from sin by many hidden forms of desire for contrition and for God's forgiveness without any sacrament (cf. qq. 74, 123) and, indeed, without any explicit reference to Christ or clear profession of faith (cf. qq. 161, 162). It is possible to be forgiven by God, as it is possible to worship God without knowing anything of the Christian community.

As an ordinary human thing, however, forgiveness, like worship, has to do with our life together. God's forgiveness comes to us sacramentally and visibly when we are forgiven and accepted and, in the name of Christ, welcomed back from grave sin by the whole people of God. Through this sacrament, we share not only in the forgiven but also in the forgiving Church. True contrition is hardly compatible with a positive refusal to respond to this loving offer of reconciliation.

Why the priest? Because by ordination the bishop or priest is authorized to represent the whole people of God at this moment of reconciliation, to speak in the name of the whole Church, and thus, in the name of Christ himself, to accept us and to proclaim to us and assure us of our forgiveness and new life (cf. qq. 82, 97).

8. Given that to use or to intend to use nuclear weapons is always unjust, we may ask whether it follows that the manufacture and deployment of them is also unjust. In this matter, opinion in the Church is, at present, divided. Some hold that the intention involved in holding these weapons is not to use them but to deter their use. Others hold that this does involve an intention to use them in certain conditions, such as retaliation. The former hold that the policy of deterrence can be just and consistent with the Gospel provided that it is simply a stage on the way to nuclear disarmament; the latter that it must always be unjust and inconsistent with the Gospel. Both agree that, given that such weapons exist, it is a primary duty to seek practical means of nuclear disarmament.

9. Note that this includes all God's creatures that are capable of suffering, not simply human beings. We cannot exercise the virtue of justice toward irrational animals for they are not, even potentially, fellow citizens either of secular society or of the kingdom of God. But we must exercise the virtues of gentleness and compassion toward them because they are fellow sentient beings.

Index

Note: The numbers indicated refer to questions, not page numbers.

The Daughters of St. Paul operate book and media centers at the following addresses. Visit, call or write the one nearest you today, or find us on the World Wide Web, www.pauline.org.